THE AMAZING LIFE OF

PAULA

10,000 MILES OF MIRACLES

PAULA LINDEMANN

authorHOUSE

AS TOLD TO
BECKY WHITE

authorHOUSE

AuthorHouse™
1663 Liberty Drive, Suite 200
Bloomington, IN 47403
www.authorhouse.com
Phone: 1-800-839-8640

© 2008 Paula Lindemann and Becky White. All rights reserved.

No part of this book may be reproduced, stored in
a retrieval system, or transmitted by any means
without the written permission of the author.

First published by AuthorHouse 3/19/2008

ISBN: 978-1-4343-5841-7 (sc)

Printed in the United States of America
Bloomington, Indiana

This book is printed on acid-free paper.

HER STORY OF SURVIVAL
THROUGH THE TURMOIL
OF WWII IN EUROPE

Dedication

I would like to dedicate this book to my God who has held onto me and never let me go. I have had so many pitfalls and made so many blunders, but He stayed right with me and pulled me out each time. He came to save all of us and forgive us for all our shortcomings. I praise His holy name for the great sacrifice He made at Gethsemane and Calvary.

I also dedicate this book to my family; my son Bobby and his wife Debbie who have stood with me and taken care of me after my accident; to Becky White who encouraged me to and then helped me write this book; Dr. Lisa Lanham who opened the door for me to have this opportunity; my dear friends who are so helpful to me: Chuck and Dianne, Joe and Cheryl, Sammie and Jim, Dorothy and Lloyd, and so many other beautiful and caring friends in and out of my church – just too many to mention here.

Thank you all and may the Lord bless you!

Paula Lindemann

INTRODUCTION

By Becky White

About two years ago while I was still living in Florida, I heard about a guest speaker who had been invited to the church my husband and I had served several years ago, the Mt. Olive United Methodist Church in Columbus, Indiana. One of our old and dear friends emailed us and said that this lady spoke for about two hours and the audience sat mesmerized, unaware of how much time had passed while she told of her experiences of leaving home at 12 years old, traveling by herself to escape the ravages of WWII in Europe, escaping from a refugee camp, surviving air raids, narrowly escaping death many times, and rescuing her scattered family from the Russian front in Germany.

I had no idea at that time that my husband and I would be called to return to serve the Mt. Olive church some two years later. We hadn't been back long when the congregation asked this lady to come back for a service to once again share some of her fascinating stories of faith and survival in unbelievable circumstances. Sitting there listening to her, I, too, was mesmerized by her story. After the service, I asked her if she had written a book about her experiences. Her answer was, "No, but I have always wanted to."

Well, thus began a relationship between storyteller and transcriber. She spoke her story on a portable cassette recorder and I transcribed it.

Paula's story is an extraordinary one of a remarkable young lady who survived life during a crucial time in history few first-hand witnesses are still alive to tell about. Neither of us claim to be writers, by any stretch of the imagination. This book is a simply written true account of an amazing lady named Paula as told to an amazed listener named Becky. Together we have spent countless hours getting her story into this book. Neither of us had any idea what an all-consuming project this would become for both of us.

We trust that after reading this book you will be unable to forget the incredible life of Paula and how the Lord has granted her ten thousand miles of miracles through bombs, bunkers, bayonets, the big brown house, a boat, betrayal, blessings and now a book!

CONTENTS

Chapter One
Zipserland 1
Chapter Two
Leutschau and Prague 19
Chapter Three
 Complete Chaos in Europe 25
Chapter Four
The Big Brown House in Zeidler 35
Chapter Five
Schmollnitz 54
Chapter Six
Sudetenland, Marienbad 65
Chapter Seven
Back to Prague 78
Chapter Eight
St. John, New Brunswick, Canada 84
Chapter Nine
America Pennsylvania 90
Chapter Ten
Columbus, Indiana 101
Chapter Eleven
Visiting Home Again 110

Chapter One

Zipserland

"SLOVAKIAN PARADISE"
Our beautiful little valley in Slovakia

They say it was about, well, nobody exactly knows, but some say 800, some say 600 years ago when my forefathers migrated from Saxony in East Germany to the little land of Slovakia. And while many said it was because of religious persecution, nobody knows exactly why they came to this beautiful valley in little Slovakia called Zipserland, which means "Slovakian Paradise."

My forefathers settled in a little town called Schwedler. A beautiful, crystal clear river called Gollnitz ran right through our town of about 2,000 people where everybody knew everybody.

On our little farm we didn't have drinking water. We had a certain well we used for just the cattle where we would lower a bucket on a chain and then bring it back up with water to pour in the troughs. That water seemed clear and clean to me, but we didn't drink it. I really don't know why.

The drinking well we shared with our neighbors was located between our houses down a little steep, a few meters away from our house, and then through a corridor about 25 feet long. We would carry our buckets to the well, lower them down, fill them with water, and then carry them back home.

On January 30th, 1921, it was 15 degrees below zero with about three feet of snow on the ground when a very pregnant young woman named Susanna went down the steep for a bucket of drinking water. When she was about halfway home with the water, she dropped the bucket. Her baby decided to enter the world right then and there. Susanna was about 20 feet from the house, holding her baby in, and yelling for the neighbors to call for the mid-wife. By the time the mid-wife came, I was born. They named me Paula, a Latin expression meaning "Small."

In looking back on my life and everything I have been through, I think that was the first attempt from the adversary, Satan, to get me, and I now know it was the first of more than 10,000 miles of miracles that I would experience.

When I was four years old, there was a Sunday when my Aunt Molly was getting married and we were all dressed up for the event. Well, the night before, there had been a terrible storm and the mud was thick and deep around our house. I got mud all over my shoes, so I went down to the river to try to clean them off. I slipped and fell into that swollen and swift river.

On the other side of the river was a sawmill and one of the men there looked up and saw my red skirt floating in the water. He yelled to the others, "Hey, look, there's something or someone in the river. It looks like a child's skirt or something. We'd better go see what it is!"

Like I said, the river was carrying me along so swiftly and it took them all working together to latch onto me. They pulled me up on the shore and turned me upside down to try to get all the water out of my lungs. They were able to reach the doctor who lived nearby and rush him to the scene. He examined me but told them he thought it was too late and that I was already gone. They took me home where my folks laid me on a bed and tended to me. I eventually came around and once again my young life was spared.

We had our own national anthem there in Schwedler. We spoke high (pure) German in school and in public, but at home we spoke with our own unique dialect. We don't know exactly where our dialect came from, but the Germans didn't understand most of it.

We were raised to ourselves, so to speak. Most of the people were farmers then, so it was all farmland with no pollution until some time later when factories moved into the bigger cities nearby.

We lived from the land there in our little Schwedler and were surrounded by the most gorgeous forest. Some of the firs and spruces were 150 feet high. The floor of the forest was amazingly beautiful from fruit berries growing abundantly. There was every kind of fruit you could imagine: raspberries, gooseberries, blackberries, strawberries. The blueberries were so abundant that when they were in bloom, there was a magnificent purple hue cast throughout the forest.

As children, we would grab a bowl after school and take a little time to pick and eat that wonderful fruit and berries all season.

We children picked all the berries for the marmalade we made in kettles. We would have jars after jars of good marmalade to last us through the winter. I liked especially the rosehip and blueberry marmalades. The rosehips were considered to be very healthy and we would pick them by the sacks full. The blueberries were good for the eyes.

We had fruit trees, too. We had plum trees, two cherry trees, two apple trees -one especially big one in the front of our house - and a pear tree behind the pig sty that would produce the most beautiful, tasty pears. And there was one pear tree that bore wee little pears. One bite and the whole pear was gone.

I don't know what they were called, but I remember they were so tasty! We lived simply, and as I said, from the land and I don't recall there being much sickness.

As children, we didn't have much time to play, but when we did, we played hopscotch. None of our ground was paved, so when it would rain, the mud would be up to five inches high. We would have to wash our shoes with a bucket full of water to try to get all that mud off.

Families depended on everybody in the household, from the youngest to the oldest, to help with the chores. So we were always busy and therefore tired at night. It was a good life, very harsh and hard in so many ways, but a good life. We always seemed to have enough to eat, and it was good food, too.

I was just a little girl then and I remember so many things that happened in my time. I remember when we first put electricity in the barn. We had cows and oxen, pigs, geese, ducks, and chickens. We had all our own meat, our own produce, a big root cellar with a huge barrel full of sauerkraut that was the best thing you could ever taste. We all worked hard and stored everything we needed for the winter.

My mother would bake 12 eight-pound loaves of bread every two weeks for our family, and we would eat most of those 12 loaves by the time she would bake again. However, there were many people much poorer than we were and we gave a lot of our bread away. It seemed to me that it was the best bread ever. I couldn't imagine there could be anything like it anywhere else in world.

We worked hard as children. Today it would probably be called child abuse. We got beaten if we were bad and sometimes we didn't even know why we got a swat. There was no softness or spoken love and affection. I never heard my mother say "I love you." I don't ever remember being hugged or kissed. In fact, my mother told me I was ugly.

When I was six years old, school started at 8:00. We had to get up at 5:30 in the morning to help in the three barns full of animals, plus the pigs. We had to get the manure out, put new bedding down for the cattle, and help with the milking.

Then we had to help make breakfast and wash the dishes. We had two big bowls for the dishes, one filled with real hot water. We used something we called "soda" which was kind of a clear soap that was harsh on our hands. That's how we washed the dishes.

We cooked on a stove that had three burners. On the holes, there were three rings. If we wanted to cook slowly, we took just the small ring out. If we wanted to cook more quickly, we took out the second ring. And if we wanted to really cook fast, we took out the third ring. The pots would get pitch black from the smoke, so we had to take them to the river so we could scrub the bottoms with fine sand.

When we did our laundry, we boiled our clothes in a big kettle. Then we would take the clothes to the crystal clear water at the river to rinse and hang them up to dry.

As kids, we had to practically steal time to do our homework. I see so many children today who have so much free time and seem to have everything. You have to tell them a hundred times to do their homework. Then it's bedtime and they say they are too tired to do it. This was not an option for my son when I was raising him. We would do what we called "drilling" and if he didn't know the answers, he was sent back to the books at least once and sometimes twice.

We were never allowed to tell our parents that we

were too tired to do our homework. That was simply unacceptable when I was a child. My mother would just look at us sometimes and we knew what she expected us to do. We never talked back to our parents. **<u>Never</u>**.

I heard a sermon the other day on the fifth commandment: honor your father and mother. I don't see that in our society today, but we really did honor our parents. We obeyed and did what we were expected to do, both at home and in school. Sometimes we truly barely had time for our homework, but we did it. That was not just our family, but everybody in the whole little valley. Children honored elders.

I was never in the "Hitler Youth" program, but we all knew what Adolph Hitler taught. He taught that young people were to honor their parents and elders. If we traveled on a bus or a train and saw an older person standing, we got up and offered them our seat. If we saw somebody walking by carrying a heavy load, we were expected to help him carry that load. People don't believe that Hitler taught that, but he did.

Germany was in good shape under Hitler's early leadership. Everyone seemed to have everything they needed and it was said that there was no unemployment or prostitution in the land.

It was under Hitler's reign that all the power lines in Germany were buried underground.

It was also during Hitler's early leadership that the 90-mile high-speed super highway, the Autobahn, was opened in 1935.

Then Hitler got power-crazy, and as history now shows, his actions brought inconceivable devastation to millions.

The year when I was six years old, the summer had been particularly dry and we didn't have enough hay for the cattle for the winter. We had to go up to a mountain called Buchwald where there was luscious grass and beautiful springs everywhere. It took three hours by oxen and hay wagon to get up the mountain and we had to make several trips to get enough hay to last through the winter.

My dad always woke me up early in the morning to go with him to help. I would cry and ask him to get someone else to go with him. It was so early and I was still sleepy. He would tell me to bring my blanket and sleep on the way up, or I could walk behind him. So, I'd get up and ride in the wagon.

When we got up the mountain, my dad would mow the grass and I would go behind him and spread it out. It was still dark when we would finish with the mowing and spreading of the grass.

When the sun came out and reflected on that freshly cut and deeply green grass, it was a beautiful sight. I would turn the grass four times during the day so that by late afternoon it would be dry enough for us to load onto the wagon.

I would be on the wagon loading the grass while my dad would pass it to me with a pitchfork. He always said that when I loaded it, it was better than what anyone else could do. When others would load it, they would always lose some on the rough and rocky way back down the hill. I guess that's why he would wake me up to go with him on those early mornings.

After the wagon was loaded, he would cut down a tree and use it to hold the wagon back from the oxen as we made our way back down that steep mountainside. With the little weight I had then, as a small child, I had to sit on that tree that was bound to the wagon to help hold it back. I was black and blue by the time we got down the hill and I got off that tree.

As I mentioned before, there was a forest near our house and we could take our cattle to graze there during those dry summers. To get to that part of the forest would take about three hours.

I took the cattle to forest to graze many times during my childhood. I would take a pillow, a blanket and some food and spend the entire weekend there, just me and the cattle. Friday evening I made my camp and went back home on Sunday evening. The cattle would stay nearby while grazing. If they did start to stray, I would call them and they would come right back.

Sometimes I felt that I could talk with those oxen and cows and horses. In the spring, when we plowed the fields, I would tell them to go right, and they would go right. I would tell them to go left, and they would go left. I had a big apron full of grain and would sow grain like the farmers mentioned in the Bible.

I recall one particular weekend when I was about seven years old that I took the cattle to the forest to graze. It was beautiful weather and the forest was just gorgeous. At night I made a big fire and the cattle would all come close around.

I ate a good supper, bread and butter and fruit. There were little wells in the wild with water as clear as crystal where I would kneel down for a drink.

One night the cattle woke me up and I heard little twigs breaking. When the cattle felt danger, they would make a certain noise, and they made that noise that night. I knew something was going on. They all were standing up, none of them would lie down. Suddenly I saw an image through the flame of the fire. No more than 20 feet away was a big bear!

Sometimes woodworkers from the forest would stop by our house and visit my dad. I had heard one of them tell a story of encountering a bear in the forest once. He said he took a hot stick out of his campfire, swung it at the bear and scared it away. I remembered that story and pulled a big hot stick from my fire, swung at that bear, and believe it or not, that bear went away. And also, believe it or not, I wasn't afraid to go back to sleep.

I laid back down and looked up at the sky, the moon, the stars and those high lovely trees, and my, what an awesome sight that was. I didn't know anything about God at that time in my life, but in those moments of childhood ignorance and innocence, I surely knew *of* Him.

It seems I was never afraid of anything.

There were some evenings when my dad and the men in our little town would gather around to spit and talk. I don't know what it was about that spitting they did, but I didn't like it. I vividly remember one particular evening when I was about five years old and I heard some of those men make comments about me to my dad, "That little girl is not afraid of even the Devil!"

When I was 12 years old, my dad said to me, "If I were you, I'd get away from here as soon as I could." I had always worked so hard and would walk as far as my little legs would carry me to help out, so I just could not understand why he would say that. Did he want me to go away? Why? I just didn't know.

It was somewhat customary during this time for the older children, usually girls, to leave home at a young age. My cousin, Clair, had done so. They called it "serving". Still, I was somewhat hurt and confused as to why my father would want me to leave, but I trusted his judgment and decided it was best for me to leave home and go on my own.

Chapter Two

Leutschau and Prague

I was born in 1921. When the war started in 1933, I left home and went by train to a beautiful town called Leutschau, about 40 miles from home.

There were a lot of Jewish people living there and I worked for a couple who had a small department store where you could buy almost anything. Since they were not permitted under Jewish law to do any kind of work on the Sabbath, I would even shut the electric lights off for them.

On Friday they would cook a pot of beans with chicken, spices, and vegetables in it and take it to the town kitchen where everybody else would bring their pots of beans. They would put it all in one big oven. Then on the Sabbath, somebody who was not Jewish would turn the oven on. It would take many hours for it all to cook and by mid-afternoon everyone would enjoy a great meal. They called it Schont and I remember it tasted so very good.

A few years ago when I had the privilege of traveling to Israel, there was a lady on the plane and we talked about Schont. When she got home, she sent me her recipe. I made it once, but since I don't eat real chicken, I used soy chicken; and while the Schont was good, it was not nearly as good as I remember it being in those days when I had left home at 12 years old for Leutschau and worked for those Jewish people.

There were a lot of travelers coming through Leutschau. One day as I was out shopping, a lady with a family approached me wondering if I knew of anybody who would go to Prague and be a nanny to her children. I asked her when she would be going back and she told me. I told her that I would be glad to take the position as nanny to her children, but that I needed to give two weeks notice to the people I was presently working for. She said that would be okay, that she would send me the money for the train and pick me up in Prague at the Wilson train station.

So I left Leutschau and went to Prague, about 600 miles from home. I liked it there and enjoyed my role as a nanny. The children went to preschool and I helped them, then I would take them to the park every afternoon. I cooked, cleaned, and washed and pretty soon was doing most everything.

The bed sheets in those days were not as fine as we have now. When they were wet they were like tin. My little hands were bleeding from washing them on a board, as we did in those days, but I did it all and went to school at night. Caring for the children, keeping up with the housework, going to school, plus learning a new language was hard, especially in light of the fact that I was about 13 or 14 years old at the time and far away from home and family.

My whole life was very harsh and hard. It seemed I was always alone and had nobody to ask which way to go and which way to come and how and what. As I said, it was hard, but the Lord helped me so much, even though I didn't know Him then.

In our home there was no religion. There was very harsh talk, cussing and swearing. We had a beautiful Bible that sat on our dining room table. It was dusted every Saturday, but nobody ever looked in it. We had several little framed writings with flowers and verses from the Bible hanging on our walls. I always liked them, but the Bible was never read. We never prayed, even when we ate. It was just nothing like I got to know when I became a true Christian.

The city of Prague had the most fascinating restaurants and hotels. There was a vegetarian restaurant on Wenzels Platz, which means a great wide street.

The idea of a vegetarian restaurant piqued my curiosity, so I decided I would go there one day when I was off work to find out what this vegetarian food was like. As I was walking down the street toward the restaurant, behold I saw Sonja Henney, the famous figure skater! She was very petite, like a doll, and of course she was Swedish and knew German. I talked to her a little and found that she was going to the vegetarian restaurant, too. So we walked there together and I was privileged to eat lunch with her. She was such a sweet person and I was so proud that I had met her! It was just wonderful. The food was so very good, too, and I fell in love with the desserts.

There was a beautiful, big dance hall in Prague which was located just across the street from the vegetarian restaurant. On Saturday evenings German music would be featured, and all the German people from that area would go there. I loved the ballroom dancing and had such fun. Sometimes I stayed out a little too late which wasn't good for me because I was about 14 years old and had to get up early the next morning and work hard all day again. But, I did it, and I really enjoyed that.

There were also wonderful movie houses in Prague. Shirley Temple's movies played there, as well as stars such as Hans Moser and Willie Birgel, and oh, they were wonderful movies! I used to just love them. When I became a Christian, the only things I felt I had to give up were dancing and movies. I didn't see anything wrong with it then, and there wasn't…. not like today. I never really cared for make-up and jewelry. I never bought lipstick in my life. I just didn't care for it, even when I was not yet a Christian.

Chapter Three
Complete Chaos in Europe

By now everyone was on the move as the war was getting worse and worse. The Nazi's occupied almost all of Europe and were confident they were going to win this war. However, advisors and high army officials were warning Hitler to quit.

Germany had three fronts against them: Africa, Russia, and America with the American allies. Germany was losing staggering numbers of men fighting against these fronts, and since there were so few men left to send, by 1944 Hitler was using 14 and 15 year old boys on the front lines.

Bombs were destroying the trains that brought food and supplies to those soldiers. At that time they would also send alcohol for the young soldiers to drink to keep them from freezing. But, again, the supply trains were being bombed and therefore a massive amount of young soldiers, boys really, were dying at an alarming rate.

I went from place to place, not able to stay too long anywhere without having to move again. I liked best a beautiful little town called Schonlinde, which means "beautiful linden tree."

In 1942, I was in Rumburg and worked in a quaint dress shop where I modeled skirts and blouses, which was what I loved to wear. The store was called Appelt, and was just like a little castle. The store owner, Mrs. Appelt, was such a gracious and pretty lady. Sometime later I heard that she died after what the Russian soldiers did to her.

I left Rumburg, and came to a beautiful little place in the mountains called Zeidler. Try as I may, I don't recall how I got to Zeidler or why I went there, but later I would realize that the Lord must have prepared this all for the job he had ahead for me.

I went to Reichenberg, which means "Rich Mountain" and became friends with some people who were Seventh Day Adventists. They had a daughter about my age and we got acquainted. She asked me if I would go to church with her on Saturday. Back where I grew up, Saturday was a very, very busy day. We went to school on Saturdays, and after school we cleaned house and did our chores.

I wondered why she would go to church on Saturday. I asked her if she was Jewish and she said that she was a Seventh Day Adventist. I know what that means today. If you become a Seventh Day Adventist, you become a spiritual Israelite, according to the Bible.

They observed the Sabbath on Saturday. I went to her church with her all of the three Sabbaths that

I was there.

From there I went back to Rumburg. There was a little Seventh Day Adventist church in Warnsdorf, about 10 miles from Rumburg, so I went on the bus to Warnsdorf and attended that church for Bible Study Classes. I studied from July until I was baptized December 12th, 1942.

As I said before, we never had any religion in our home. There were only Lutherans and Catholics in our community, and my father was the treasurer of the Lutheran church. There was some hatred between the two religions. Many of the children made ugly jokes and remarks about one another. Mostly though, we were able to put our differences aside and be good neighbors.

When I wrote home that I had become a Seventh Day Adventist, I was told that it was one of the worst things I could do, worse than being a criminal. It was probably because of the issue of observing Saturday as the Sabbath instead of Sunday. They really did not know what Adventists were. Even today some people call us a cult, but if they would search the scripture they would find that we worship as our Lord and his apostles did.

It was early in 1944, before the evacuations started, when I went back home for my Uncle Martin's wedding. It was the first time I had been home since 1942. When I was walking from the railroad station down the street to my home, some of the local women walked behind me. I had a suitcase and they must have recognized me. All of a sudden, they moved out in front of me and said, "How dare you show your face in this town again!" and then spit on me.

In that culture, if you were born into a Lutheran or Catholic family, you were expected to remain a Lutheran or Catholic for the rest of your life. For you to have a choice in the matter was not an option, and any other way was considered rebellion. My family was Lutheran, and I was supposed to be Lutheran, no matter what I thought or felt.

The preacher at my home church was nice to me. Evidently he, like so many others had told me, agreed with me about the Sabbath, but their church taught another way. You remember it says in the Bible that the Bereans were "more noble." When they heard the apostles preach, especially Paul, they went home and checked if what they had heard was in the scrolls, and that was why they were called more noble.

A lot of people are content to just stay where they are. Think of Martin Luther in his days. As long as he lived, he did a lot to reform and to protest. A "protestant" means to "protest" something, but you don't hear of many folks in the churches protesting much today.

We need to know the Bible, study it, and protest against any untruth being taught to millions of people. We need to go back to the scripture, like the Bereans, and see if what we are being taught is so.

The other day I heard a sermon that really did something for me. I cried out to God, "Father, please teach me how to live a life that pleases you. I don't want to be lost with the wicked. I want to honor you. You left heaven and all the glory you had, dear Savior. You came down here to earth and suffered and died for us all. Even if it would have been only for me, you would still have come and suffered and died."

I contemplated on how they treated the Lord like a common criminal and what he suffered for us. Even though it is described in the Bible, it still is mind-boggling what he did for us. When He soon comes in the clouds, we'll be rid of evil and He will take us home to Heaven to live with him forever, and ever, and ever. I really don't understand what forever is, but that sounds just marvelous to me. I want to be ready when Jesus comes. If I'm still living, I want to look up to Heaven and say, "Lo, this is our Lord. I have waited for Him and He will save me."

That will be the most glorious and yet most terrible day the whole universe has ever seen. I think we all should get busy for the time is short and the events happening in this world tell us that Jesus is very near. Today is your day of salvation. Tomorrow you and I may not be here. You need to be ready today. The Bible tells us we should not worry about tomorrow; that tomorrow will take care of itself. Seek ye first the kingdom of Heaven and all those things you need, God knows, will be given to you.

In 1942 and 1943, even though I didn't make much money, I sent most of it home so my folks could remodel their old farmhouse. By early 1944, when I went home for my Uncle Martin's wedding, they finally had it completed.

While I was back home for the wedding, I visited with some neighbors, Mr. and Mrs. Fabry, who lived about three houses down from the house where I had grown up. Mr. Fabry had been a shoemaker and we had often bought shoes from him while we were growing up.

Mrs. Fabry and I were sitting in her yard and she said to me: "Paula, you know why your mother hates you so much, don't you? She is jealous of you and your dad because he always preferred that you go everywhere with him." Mrs. Fabry had also talked to my dad and he had told her that he preferred me because the work I did with him was just perfect.

For the first time in my life, I was able to understand why my father had advised me to leave home at such an early age and why my mother hated me. It was ridiculous in my mind that my mother would be so jealous. After all, I was just a small child!

As fate would have it, that was the last time I was home.

Chapter Four
The Big Brown House In Zeidler

In March of 1944, my distant cousin Michael, who was in the German Air Force, had a few days of leave and came to visit me for a day or two. I thought I would go with him to visit his folks. We traveled about two hours by train into Aussig-Schreckenstein, on the River Elbe, when we had to stop because there had been an air raid the night before and the tracks had to be repaired. We were told it would take until about 2:00 that afternoon for the repairs to be complete and then we could continue traveling.

On one side of the Elbe River was a medical factory where we were told that Bayer aspirin had originated. On the other side was the railroad, a highway, a mountain with a restaurant on it, and a farm. The mountain was full of people on this beautiful March day. The sky was blue without a cloud and the weather was very pleasant. At around noon my cousin Michael said, "There's an air raid coming! Let's run into the woods!"

I said, "Michael, I don't hear anything. How do you know there is an air raid coming?"

He again said, "Paula, there's an air raid coming and it's the American planes." He even knew the sound of the American planes from a distance and could differentiate the American bombers from the British bombers. The American and British Air Forces were bombing day and night alternately.

By the time I quit arguing with him, the sky was black with planes. They dropped one or two of the big bombs there and destroyed everything, the restaurant, the farm, the medical factory. The air was black with smoke and the odor was overwhelming!

Two or three hours later when the air cleared

a bit, we could see pieces and limbs of cattle and people hanging from the branches of the trees and on the fences. The railroad tracks had blown all over everywhere.

After the big bombs, they dropped phosphor bombs that looked like walking sticks. Half of it seemed to be red foil and half silver. If you would get a phosphor bomb in your back, it would literally cook you from the inside out. Water wouldn't put the fire out. It took a special chemical to extinguish the fire.

There was complete devastation. For Michael and I to be so close to where the bombs were dropped and to live through it and have no injuries was nothing other than a miracle. Once again my life had been spared.

Michael still had a couple of days on leave and decided to try to walk the rest of the way to his home. We hugged, said our goodbyes and wished each other good luck. He headed back home and I started the long walk back to where I was living.

I never saw or heard from Michael again. To this day I don't know if he made it home or not.

There were hundreds of people walking my direction and I heard them talking about seeing people in the Elbe River cooking like a roast. As I said before, water wouldn't put out the fire from those stick-like bombs.

By this time in 1944, the war was causing complete chaos all over Europe. I found out the German army had evacuated the mothers and children from our old homestead in August because the Russian front was rapidly advancing to that area. No one seemed to know where the evacuees had gone.

Everyplace was full of refugees. There was hardly any place to put people anymore. And on top of it, so many areas had been destroyed by bombs and the bombing kept getting worse and worse day and night.

While I was still in Zeidler I heard that my mother, my youngest sister, and my only brother were in a camp in Linz, Austria. I asked the mayor of Zeidler if I could go by train to try to find some of my people and bring them back with me. He said "Sure you can go, but where are we going to put them? The only place with any room is the big brown house."

I went to Linz looking for my family and discovered that they were scattered in different refugee camps all over the place. News spread to me from different sources saying they thought my mother and siblings were in Linz, and that my grandparents, and several others from my family were in Katovice, Poland.

I found my mother, my brother and youngest

sister there in Linz. The leader of the camp had been a teacher at my homestead. He had been given the responsibility for all the people at this camp and since I didn't have any official documentation as to where I was taking them, he didn't want to release them to me. I had an awful struggle and he delayed us for two days, but we finally got away and headed for the train nearby.

While we were going to the train station, there was an air raid. I thought for sure we were going to die. Not far from the train station was a bunker about four feet thick in cement where you could take shelter during an air raid. We quickly went in. It was just terrible. It seemed like the whole bunker was moving and throwing people around. There was screaming and swearing, cussing and praying! Finally it was over and we came out to see complete pandemonium. Those dreadful big bombs that destroy everything had been dropped.

Finally we got on the train and headed for Poland to find the rest of our family before heading back to the big brown house in Zeidler. To tell you the truth, it was all so traumatic that I don't remember how we got to Poland.

I found my grandmother, grandfather, and many of my other relatives at a camp in Katovice.

I had been away about a month, and ended up bringing 32 people back with me to the big brown house in Zeidler, that little town in the mountains that I mentioned earlier – also called the "Mineral Mountains."

I can't recall certain things like where we stayed or what we ate all that time. It all happened so quickly and we were in several air raids with such turmoil and chaos everywhere. I was 23 years old and what an experience that was!

The brown house was two and half stories. It

was an impressive building which had been the Nazi headquarters for that area. There were Nazi paintings and slogans written all over the walls.

The people who were gone from the area had left some furniture and possessions behind in their houses, so the Mayor told us to get beds and whatever we needed. This was in the winter of 1944. The Russians destroyed much of it later on when they came through.

Zeidler was nothing but farms, beautiful villas and houses. The people who lived there were wealthy from taking care of the mountains. I had worked for awhile for the president of the Mineral Mountains. He and his family had a lovely villa, but they left late in 1944 to get away from the Russians.

My father and the men from our homestead were evacuated in November of 1944. Somehow they found out where we were and joined us sometime that winter.

The winter was very cold and a lot of people who had lived in Zeidler were leaving. I wondered what we were going to do. I was just thankful to have us all together under one roof. It was sure better than being spread out all over in refugee camps.

Spring came and there was work to be done in the fields before planting during March and April.

The Russian front was coming closer and closer and there was hardly anyplace to go anymore. Refugees were everywhere and it was so frustrating wondering what to do. Should we go or should we stay. Nobody could make up their mind.

On the 3rd of May in 1945, late in the evening, the Russians came into our town. Everybody was screaming and running. Where could we hide and what could we do? Since I spoke a little bit of Russian, some mothers frantically asked me to help them. They wanted to know where to hide their young daughters. Several people suggested putting them in basements or behind a pile of coal or a pile of wood with a pipe coming out so they could have air. All kind of things were suggested to do.

With all the panic and fear and screaming, I was so glad I was a Christian. All of the 32 people I had brought back with me were in that big brown house and I prayed, "Lord, what am I going to do with all these people?"

There were 18 steps leading up to the house. I went down and opened the big door so the soldiers wouldn't destroy it with their bayonets. As I came back upstairs to the hall, there wasn't a soul there. They had all gone up to the attic to hide from the Russians.

I asked them "What am I going to do now?"

My dad said, "You'll do okay. You speak Czech

and you can talk to them." Yes, I spoke Czech, but those soldiers were Russians and I didn't know that much of the Russian language. He encouraged me to go downstairs and try to deal with them. It was almost funny to think that there were three men among the bunch who were over six feet tall but they sent me, a 95 pound petite young lady to deal with the Russian soldiers. I guess my dad had faith that I could handle the situation. So I went down to the kitchen to see if there was some food I could give them when they came.

All of a sudden I heard them outside. I stood at the top of the hallway stairs and saw eight soldiers. One was a colonel. Seven were Russian and one was a Czech. My fear heightened when I remembered there were four or five young girls upstairs, but I managed to greet them nicely. I invited the soldiers into the big kitchen where there was a long beautiful table. They stank and were so filthy and hungry. They had destroyed and raped everything and everyone in their paths.

It was about midnight or 1:00 in the morning when they came. We sat and talked and I asked them if I could offer them something to eat. They agreed as they were hungry. All I had was a big loaf of bread a farmer had given me, and butter, milk and water. Food was scarce everywhere since it was spring and all the winter supplies were all gone.

I put everything I had on the table with plates and knives and glasses for milk and water. One soldier said, "I don't want any water; I want vodka!"

I said, "I'm sorry, I don't have any vodka. You'll have to drink water or milk."

"I don't want any milk!" he demanded.

"Well, I'm sorry, I have nothing else."

They drank every single drop of our milk and

water and ate every morsel of that whole loaf of bread. It was all gone.

One soldier asked me, "Where are your folks? You don't live here alone, do you?"

I said, "No, they're in the attic hiding from you. They were afraid you might hurt them."

I prayed all night in my heart, "Lord, protect us and let your Holy Spirit work on the hearts of those men."

We talked about a lot of things. One man cried and said, "We are supposed to go and kill people that have never done anything to us. We never met them, we don't know them and we're supposed to kill them."

One of the soldiers said to me, "I'm going to take you with me to Russia. The Germans killed my wife."

I said in my heart, "Oh Lord, I don't want to go to Russia! Please keep me safe!"

And the Lord was so good to us. Nothing happened to any of our girls or me. Believe it or not, at 8:00 in the morning, those eight Russians left the big brown house.

They were in our town about three days and then most of them left. We learned that several of the young girls had been found and raped. When most of the soldiers had left, the girls were taken to a nearby village where there were doctors available to care for them.

That last day some of the soldiers came with a truck and brought us stuff we hadn't seen in several years in Germany, or probably anywhere. Stuff like sugar, cigarettes, all kind of goods you couldn't get except on the black market. They had probably found it all in some of the vacated homes of the wealthy and brought it to us. When they finally were leaving, I was hiding and hoping the one who wanted to take me back to Russia wouldn't find me. The neighbors said he didn't come by looking for me.

They came there on the 3rd of May and on the 5th of May, 1945, the war was over. Most of them left on the 6th of May.

There were just a few, however, who stayed in the area. They had their weapons and began acting pretty high and mighty. There was one in particular who was quite obnoxious and I didn't like him at all. One day I smarted off to him and he pulled me to his side and put a gun to my head. My mother came down the steps and saw what was happening and screamed. This startled him and he let me go. Maybe I should have been, but I was not afraid of anything.

So what were we going to do now? We stayed

there in the big brown house in Zeidler. Most of the men worked on the farms and the women worked in the barns and kitchens and helped plant gardens. We had a real good time that spring, until rumors spread that there was a train going to our old homestead, and that whoever wanted to go back home could go on that train.

We all sat down and I said, "We are not going on that train! That's going east! Our home is now occupied by Communist people from who knows where!" Most of the German people were gone, although a few had stayed. I adamantly argued that we go west somewhere, not east again. "We ran away from the east and now you want to go back?" I asked.

So we argued back and forth as I begged not to go east. I thought maybe we could find a new place somewhere in the west to settle and start a new life. But no, they all wanted to go east, back home to

Zipserland.

In a way I didn't blame them. The men were just in their middle forties, my dad and some of the farmers. The barns and haylofts and bins were full of all kinds of grains when they were forced to leave. The root cellar was full of potatoes. There was a big barrel of sauerkraut. There were cattle in the barn for the winter and everything was there and in good supply. Then they had to leave it all: the dogs, the cats, the ducks, pigs, geese, oxen, milk cows and it must have been very hard for them. Now they just wanted to go back home.

It was November of 1944 when my dad and the men from the area had to leave home because the Communist army was so close they could hear the shooting. The winter of 1944 was the worst winter of the century in Europe.

My mother had baked some bread before the

women and children were evacuated in August, and the bread was still good in early November when the men left, but everything was frozen. So the men gnawed on that frozen bread for their food. My dad said when he and the other men were forced to leave their homes, they just started walking and kept walking in that frigid weather not knowing where they were. On the highways they saw dead horses and cattle blown up like balloons and baby carriages with frozen babies in them.

My dad was just a little guy, but he was very tough and a hard worker. I had never seen him cry before, but he cried when he told us that story.

It was very hard for him and the other men to leave their homes, and I really didn't blame them for wanting to go back. But it was already occupied by other people, hateful people.

They were all adamant about going back to our

homestead, so I gave in and finally decided to go with them.

Chapter Five

Schmollnitz

The train we had been told would take us back home was a cattle train and it was just terrible. People were told to sit on the floor. I was the only one who could speak any different language than German. I told them that if someone should open the door, please just be quiet and don't say anything because the Communists thought we were Slovakian people.

My grandmother got mad and said, "Now we can't even talk!"

I said, "Yes, you can talk, but when you hear somebody open the door, just keep quiet."

The Communists went from cattle wagon to cattle wagon, opening the doors, looking around.

Some people had a few belongings, some had very little. The Russians opened up everything and threw it all on the floor. When they found a Swastika in one of the suitcases, they knew we were Germans. I talked to them, admitted we were Germans and tried to reason with them. It was terrible for me!

At that time we were crossing a big bridge over the River Elbe. They said they were going to throw all us Germans in the river. I prayed. I prayed constantly in my heart that the Lord would help us not be drowned in the Elbe.

The train stopped several places to get some water, but there was nothing for us to eat.

Some people along the way must have found out who we were on that cattle train and where we were going, so they brought some food to us. One time the train stopped for two or three hours and even though food was scarce everywhere, people baked potatoes outside on hot coals and shared them with us. We were so very hungry and oh my, those potatoes tasted so good! I can close my eyes still today, more than 60 years later, and smell and taste those wonderful potatoes!

It was so good to have people bring us things we really needed, but it was an awful time of travel. Several days had passed and I was constantly running back and forth on the train, talking to the people, the little that I could. Some of the Communist soldiers spoke Czech and I knew the Czech language since I had lived in Prague for four years before the war when I left home so early. They finally left us alone.

In Schmollnitz the train stopped and we were told to get out. We were about 40 miles from our homestead. The Russian soldiers took us to a big camp that was surrounded by beautiful woods.

The war had just ended and there was no

government and no order. Some of the soldiers were punks that threw us into camps like criminals. They took it all on their own, and there was no police or anyone to ever check what was going on.

There was a huge building there where there were bunks with just boards for us to sleep on. This camp was just for young girls. Nearby there was another camp for mothers and children where they put my Mom and younger siblings. And there was yet a different camp for men where my Dad and the men from our family were kept.

So there we were, seven girls: three sisters and four cousins by the same name, "Groeh" all in this one camp.

There was a cigarette factory near our camp and some of the people who worked there, as well as some nearby farmers came and helped us get branches from the huge spruce and fir trees. Some of those spruce trees were 150 feet tall and beautiful wood. That was our bed, branches and needles from the trees. The farmers brought us some horse blankets, which were in terrible condition, but we were thankful to have covers.

After a few days, I woke up one morning and my green horse blanket had turned gray. It was full of lice. There were three bunk beds on top of each other and I was on the bottom, so I guess I got all the lice from the top.

Several days later, they told us we had to go into the woods to take apart the bunkers the Communists had used when they came by there. We had to get up at 3:00 in the morning and walk about 2 ½ to 3 hours through that beautiful woods, to the top of a mountain. From there you could look into Hungary.

At first it didn't seem too bad. We were young

and the walking was okay, but the work was hard. There were berries galore, all kinds of berries, so we snatched and ate berries. But other than the berries, all we had to eat for seven months was little navy beans two times a day. They were boiled in water without salt, fat, or seasoning of any kind.

After a while, we got some sort of skin condition affecting the whole body except for the wrist, hands, face and neck, which were clear. Eventually our skin became like the bark on a tree, only brown, and itched terribly. Some people scratched so hard the blood would flow. There was no hygiene whatsoever for us and no running water. There was, however, a little creek we could go to. In the cold months we would have to take a stick to break up the ice, but many times the ice was too thick to break. We used that little creek to clean ourselves the best we could. The neighbors would bring us some towels. They were very nice to us, but of course they were

Germans who had stayed there.

During that time several of us were afflicted with painful boils. At our girl's camp, several of us had a few boils. I had four. But in the men's camp, apparently they were badly affected. My father had 24 painful boils around his waist.

I was made to cook for the soldiers at our camp. There was one German soldier by the name of Stephan who was very nice to me. He would allow me to take some of the food from the kitchen, and then let me take the food to my mother and younger siblings at a camp nearby. I would pass it to her through the fence there. Stephan took me to his mother's home a couple of times and I would get a good meal.

One day we seven girls met together a little bit away in the camp. The gate was locked and we went to the farthest corner and talked. I wanted to get out of there, and suggested that somehow when the gate was open, maybe real early in the morning, we could get out. So we made a date. When the time came, I was there and ready to go. My cousin, Marie, met me inside the gate and whispered to me that none of them wanted to go.

I tried to escape by myself. Sometimes at night we all had to go outside in the fenced in yard so they could count and make sure everybody was there. This particular night they did the count and realized I was missing. They hunted me down and brought me back to the camp.

I escaped for the second time, but got caught and brought back to the camp again. This time though, the soldier who caught me beat me with the butt of his gun.

It was now November and I had no winter clothes. A lady we had helped out during the hay season while confined at that camp had made me a long sleeved blouse from an old sheet with a high neck to cover my skin disease. That was all I had. No winter shoes, no winter coat.

On the morning of November 19th, 1945, some special political event happened in Russia. I had been watching to see when the gates were opened and closed. At 1:00 that afternoon, I went out of the gate for my third attempt at escaping. There were bushes I could creep through to get to the train station. I made it this time and was able to get on the train.

I had been at the camp for seven months.

The rest of my family remained at the camps for almost two years and then were taken all the way to East Germany, by the East Sea, to a place called Mecklenburg. The other side of the East Sea was Sweden. Mecklenburg had been the bread basket for all of Germany before Germany was divided. This area was all Communists now.

Our extended family was scattered all over Mecklenburg. The remaining seven members of my immediate family were put in a 20' x 30' room in the upstairs portion of a house. The bottom of the house was a hog pen.

Years later, when I was visiting my family, they told me the story that the Mayor of their area came to visit them in that one-room upstairs dwelling and said that he had never seen such a clean and spotless place where seven people lived in such small quarters.

My sisters eventually ran away to West Germany, to the other side of The Iron Curtain and began lives there. They traveled through the wooded areas and sometimes weren't sure on which side of Germany they were. They finally found that the best way to tell East Germany, which was now occupied by the

Communists, from West Germany was that East Germany was so unkempt. The land had high weeds everywhere and was in such disarray. Also, many of the German farmers who saw them running through the woods knew where they were going and would point to them which way was west.

My brother and sister Bertha ended up staying there in Mecklenburg under Communistic reign with my parents.

Chapter Six

Sudetenland, Marienbad

So here I was on a train bound for who knows where. I heard the conductor coming, so I went into the bathroom, locked the door and stayed until I heard him leave that area. I was safe and had finally made the break from the camp in Schmollnitz, but I had never felt so lost and lonely. I had nothing to eat, didn't know where to go, and had no money.

There were two older ladies on the train who came to me and offered me a crust of bread and an apple to eat. It's amazing how good the simplest foods taste when you are so very hungry.

We traveled almost 800 miles to Sudetenland, Marienbad, which was a beautiful, beautiful city on the German border. The train stopped there and went no further. Everyone got out and scattered to their homes. They lived there, but I had no where to go.

It was about 8:00 or 9:00 in the evening and since that was the wintertime, it was pitch dark. I was shivering, hungry, filthy, and felt half-frozen.

There was a lovely big park where there were hot springs coming out of the ground and a beautiful hospital sanatorium. The city was known as a healing place where people came from all over the world for treatment of heart disease and tuberculosis.

The park was well-lit, and around the park were benches and life-sized fairy tale characters. I sat at the "Little Red Riding Hood" display, by the wolf. There I prayed to the Lord asking what to do now and where to go, telling him I was so cold and hungry.

I felt like there was a tap on my shoulder and I heard someone telling me to go to the sanatorium to see if Annie was still there. Annie was a nurse with whom I had communicated during the war. I had sent packages to her brother who was a soldier, but I hadn't thought about nor heard from Annie for a long time. I said, "Thank you Lord! Would you please let her be there?"

I went to the back door of the sanatorium and a man came out and threw something in the bushes. I asked him if he would be so kind and check to see if Annie Stich was still there. He said he would and came back out and said, "Yes, she is still here." Can you imagine how I felt?

I said, "Would you please tell her to come to the back door?" In a couple of minutes she came. It was dark in the back, and she looked at me and looked again and said, "Paula? Come in quickly so nobody will see you."

She took me in and I had my first bath in seven

months! Oh, I could hardly make myself get out of that tub! It was so warm and refreshing. I still had that disease on my skin. My skin was brown and was like the bark on a tree, but was bleeding some. That was a Thursday night.

She went to the kitchen and was able to sneak some food for me to eat, and oh, my, did that food taste good!

She gave me some winter clothes and told me that the Czechs had taken over the sanatorium and that Monday morning would be the last transport of the German doctors and nurses to go to Germany. Their train would be leaving at 4:00 a.m.

"You have to be out of here just a little after 3:00 a.m. so nobody will see you. I can't take you with us, you don't have any papers and they very strictly check everything." She wished me well and I left about quarter after three. That was the last time I ever saw or heard from Annie again.

I went back to the "Little Red Riding Hood" display in the park. I was warmer and had had something to eat and three wonderful, refreshing baths. As I heard Annie's train leaving, I prayed and thanked the Lord for what was nothing short of a miracle. It was about 20 degrees below zero and dark out.

I sat there on the park bench and watched as the sky grew brighter and lighter and the sun came up at about 8:00. I felt led to go to the police station. There was a very handsome young man with pitch black hair behind the desk. He looked up and said, "What can I do for you?"

Well, I lied and said, "I must have lost my I.D. card. I need a new I.D. to find a job and a place to live."

"Well," he said, "you'll have to write to your

hometown city hall. I need your birth certificate and your address."

"I can't do that! I need an I.D. now! Sir, if you can't give me a real one, at least give me a temporary one until I can get the papers for you," I pleaded. I could not have gotten any papers anyway since our homestead was now occupied with strange people. I wouldn't want them to know anything about me.

"I'm sorry. I can't do that!" was his answer.

Well, I walked to the door and I don't know if it was seconds or minutes, but I prayed in my heart that the Holy Spirit would touch that young man's heart and make him give me an I.D.. I could do nothing without it. I wondered where I would go. I didn't know anybody there, didn't have one cent, and was sick with that skin disease.

He probably thought I was crazy, but as I stood at the door and prayed, he got up from behind the desk, motioned for me to come and sit down, and wrote me a temporary I.D. That was about 8:30, and believe it or not, by 11:00 a.m. I had a job at the most beautiful shoe store, called Bat'a, pronounced "batcha."

There I met two girls, Vera and Maruska, who told me of housing for girls where they lived, and that next to their room was a corner room which was vacant. I believe the Lord had let that room be empty just for me. I had no suitcase, just a little bag that Annie had given me, nothing else.

That night I had a bath and a good meal. The shoe store manager, his wife, and their two little children were so nice to me, God bless their hearts. I wonder where they are now.

THE CHILDREN OF THE SHOE STORE MANAGER

After two weeks of employment, I was able to see a doctor about my skin disease. I was still wearing the long sleeved blouse that the lady back at the camp had made me, and therefore, nobody could see my arms. I found out that the doctor there was Jewish, and I prayed "Lord please don't let him find out that I am German." He examined me and said he had never seen anything like it. He asked me where I had come from. Well, I couldn't tell him that, so I just said that I must have gotten it somewhere traveling.

I couldn't tell him the truth.

In those days they had boxes made of thin wood, about 2 ½ or 3 inches high, which would hold about a pound. He gave me a box like that with an ointment inside that looked like butter to me. He also gave me some kind of liquid in a bottle. He said that every morning when I got up I should put that ointment on, cover it up, and then at night have a hot bath followed with an application of that liquid.

The first time I did that, I had to put a towel in my mouth so I wouldn't scream, and it burned so badly. It felt like I was on fire. I found out the liquid he had given me was alcohol to burn out the infection. Then the salve would soften it.

After a few days, there were clumps of stuff in the tub that had fallen off my body. It was awful and I didn't know what to do with it because I didn't want anybody to know. I don't remember what I did, but

I must have found a way to dispose of it. I did that for two months or so and finally all the scabs and scars had fallen off. Then I had holes in my body for two years while my skin healed.

It felt so good to be clear of that awful skin condition. I had felt like I had leprosy or something. During the days it just itched so much and of course I couldn't keep scratching my arms while at work. The people would have wondered what was wrong. Nobody knew anything about it until it was gone. The doctor had been so nice to me. I don't know whether he knew I was German or not, but he helped me get rid of that problem.

I loved it there in Marienbad. The shoe store was a wonderful place to work. I did errands for the manager and took his children on walks with me. I was so thankful to be making some money. I sent most of the little I made to the farmers back in Schmollnitz, who in turn took it to the camp where my mother was with my brother and youngest sister. We had no home at that time.

At the shoe store where I was working, there were three boys upstairs who made the shoes, and the girls downstairs sold them. They invited me to go boating and swimming with them, but I didn't talk much or associate with anybody for fear they would find out about my past. However, one Sunday I went with them and we were all together and talking and one guy asked if I spoke German. "Yes," I said. "I worked in Germany during the war and speak a little."

We got acquainted more and one night he broke into my room. I screamed and the girls next door heard it. He escaped and ran back to his place. After that event, he became hateful to me.

One day in June I was walking through the park to the Post Office to mail a package for the manager when seemingly out of nowhere a policeman approached me and asked me to show my I.D. This was about 10:00 in the morning. I explained that I didn't have my I.D. with me and told him that if he would come around noon I could show it to him then. The manager's children were with me, and as the policeman was leaving, I turned to see the guy who had broken into my room hiding behind a tree watching what was going on. I decided that he had figured out my situation from our conversations and had told the police about my being German.

So I turned around and went right back to the store, upstairs where the manager lived, and told him what had happened. I confessed who I was and everything.

"There is a train leaving at 12:00 for Prague," the manager said. He gave me two months salary and his wife gave me a little suitcase with nice clothes, since we were the same size. I had been there about six months. Then the manager said, "I knew you were

German when you came in that morning looking for a job."

**VERA AND MARUSKA, MY FRIENDS
AT THE SHOE STORE**

Chapter Seven
Back to Prague

I went the back way so no one could see me go to the train station. There were 15 people in line at the ticket window and I was so afraid that by the time my turn came to get a ticket, the authorities would come and take me back. What if someone had seen me going away with a suitcase?

The Holy Spirit was with me once again, as I was praying constantly. I was so glad I was a Christian; otherwise I never would have made it. I felt the Holy Spirit say, "Go to the third gentleman in line and ask him to buy you a ticket to go to Prague."

I went and said, "Excuse me sir, are you going to Prague?"

"Oh yes," he said, "that is where I am going. I

live there." When the gentleman agreed to purchase my ticket for me, I gave him the money and went out of the building to wait on the benches out by the train. I was so afraid that someone had seen me and would be coming after me. Finally we got on the train before all the other people got their tickets and somehow I felt I could talk about anything to that man. He had such a distinguished appearance about him. He had some gray hair and was very handsome.

I don't know how many hours we were on the train, but by the time we got to Prague that gentleman knew everything about me. I found out his name was Charles Kudrnka.

When we arrived in Prague, he found a little place where I could spend the first night, and by the second night I had a little apartment and a job in an umbrella factory. It is very interesting how umbrellas are made.

I had worked at the umbrella factory for several months when I heard they were hiring people at the British embassy in Prague. They needed someone who could speak both German and Czech, since there were a lot of Germans there seeking visas to get out of Czechoslovakia. I was hired and then my trouble started.

If you had anything to do with the west, or a person from the west, every move you made was watched by the Communist officials. I didn't realize they had found out where I lived.

I soon discovered they watched me go to the streetcar to get to work. They knew everything. Suddenly I started getting strange phone calls asking me to go to a movie or to a dance. I said, "I don't go to movies or dances. I'm sorry, but thank you for asking." The caller knew where I lived, where I waited for the streetcar, everything.

Every Saturday Mr. Kudrnka, the gentleman who had helped me get to Prague, took me to church. He stayed for the service with me, and I think he became an Adventist later.

I told him about the phone calls I had been getting and he told me I had better watch out for myself. Both of us were being watched, and he was getting phone calls, too. He told me to check with the embassy to obtain a visa to get out of Czechoslovakia, which I did.

It was now late summer in 1949. I escaped from the camp in Schmollnitz in 1945 and spent almost a half of a year in Marienbad in the shoe store before coming to Prague in 1946.

I received my visa and he took me to the train station. I found out that the train was barely out of No Man's Zone, the land between Czechoslovakia and Germany, when the police came and arrested him.

I passed from No Man's Zone into Germany and the Communist officials couldn't do anything to me anymore. I was safely on German soil now.

There was a train that went every single day from Germany to the Czechoslovakian border. We had made an arrangement that if something should happen, that there by a window on the train was a little slot in a certain wagon (or coupe). You could fold a letter real small and stick it in there.

There was a town nearby where the train stopped and I could check for messages from him. I found the first letter in that little slot above the window in the train.

I wrote back and a friend of his picked it up and took it to him at the jail. That was how we communicated. I found out that he was in jail almost two years for helping me escape. After that

I never heard from him again. To this day, I don't know what happened to him. I hope he'll be in the kingdom. He was so very nice and a real gentleman. The Lord surely had him at that train in Marienbad to help me.

Mr. Charles Kudrnka

Chapter Eight
St. John, New Brunswick, Canada

I had a sister in Germany and somehow we got in touch with each other. She asked me to come to where she lived, which I did. I got a job in a children's clothing factory. I liked it there and found that I could sew real well with my hands. They put me doing jobs not on the machines, but jobs that required hand-sewing, like sewing bows on the little dresses, fancy collars or buttons and things like that. I worked there for awhile and got an apartment. I was there from late summer in 1949 until 1952.

In June of 1952, there was a World Youth Congress of the Seventh Day Adventists to be held in Paris, France. Several of us from the church went and I stayed with another girl for three weeks. We had the most wonderful time.

I had a friend at the church I attended named Heddie who lived in Rheinland which was now occupied by the British. She worked for a British colonel who asked her one day if she knew of any young lady who would go to Canada as a nanny for friends he had there. The friend who was seeking a nanny was a banker and his wife worked in an office. They had adopted a four year old little girl named Andrea.

Heddie asked me one day if I would be interested in the position as nanny in Canada and I said, "Heddie, I'll go there. Have them to make out a visa."

In three weeks, on October 5th, 1952, I was on a ship leaving Bremer-Hafen, Germany, going to St. John, New Brunswick, Canada. It was a little ship called Arosa Kulm, a 23,000 ton Italian ship.

It was packed full of refugees getting out of Germany and many other countries. I was with 16 people in one cabin and as we went out of Bremer-Hafen, it was fine sailing. We went by England and the White Cliffs of Dover, and it was really beautiful.

On about the fourth or fifth day, we were hit by a terrible Atlantic storm. There were 30 foot waves on some stretches and that little ship was like a matchbox! We were a day and a half late in the St. Lawrence River to Montréal. One night it was so stormy and rough that one other man and I were the only ones who didn't get seasick and could eat. It is said that one may not get seasick for several trips across the ocean, but then get sick the next time. You just never know.

Those who were seasick couldn't get to the bathroom and were laying everywhere. In the group of 16 that I was with, I asked if anyone wanted anything to eat and they couldn't believe I was still on my feet. Many said they were so sick they wanted to die. I thought, "Oh Lord, that must be awful!"

One night was so bad that the sailors on the ship just didn't know what to do. The water was six feet high in the walkways of that little ship. That night we all thought that was going to be it for all of us. You could hear noises that sounded like the nails were coming off and that little ship was going to come apart. Finally the storm subsided and we got to the St. Lawrence River and arrived in Montréal.

I had a flight to St. John, New Brunswick where my new employers lived. I flew out the same day we arrived in Montréal, and arrived late that afternoon in New Brunswick where they were waiting for me. It was October 16th, 1952. It was all pretty scary and I was so thankful to the Lord that I was still living.

My new employers looked nice and little Andria

was so cute. I really enjoyed cooking, cleaning and taking care of Andria. It was a little hard since I didn't know English yet and could not talk with anybody. Still, in spite of the language barrier, Andria and I got along just fine.

I looked for a Seventh Day Adventist church in St John, and found one where services were held in a beautiful auditorium. I had soon made several friends and felt at home there.

I taught myself English and therefore didn't attend the local vocational school; however, a young lady from the church asked me if I would go to the school's Christmas party with her. It was there I met the man who would later become my husband. He had come from Saxony, East Germany, to a job in St. John, New Brunswick in the spring of 1952, and I came to my job there in October. He was taking a class at the vocational school to learn English. We had a nice talk and got acquainted.

In the spring of 1953, he was given an opportunity to make a lot of money by building American radar stations in Alaska. He left for Alaska in very early spring and was there from early spring until October of 1953 when he came back to St. John and took a job at a paper mill. We had many friends at the church that we attended together and were very happy.

On October 24th, 1953, we were married in our beautiful church. It was a lovely ceremony and we had such a nice time. After our marriage, he joined the church and was baptized.

I was obligated to work on my job as a nanny for a year so I could pay my employers back for my trip from Germany to Canada. I was making $40 a month.

Chapter Nine
America
Pennsylvania

I had always wanted to come to America. Both of my grandfathers were working at a steel mill in Pittsburgh, Pennsylvania. The women and children didn't want to come, so eventually my grandfathers went back to Slovakia where we had lived.

My husband and I had a sponsor near Beaver Valley, Pennsylvania, about 40 miles west of Pittsburgh. The town was called Zelienople, and a lot of German people had settled there. Apparently a pioneer family who had settled there had two girls, one named Zelie and the other Ople, and thus the name of the town become Zelienople.

On September 30th, 1954, when I was about

eight months pregnant, we flew to Pennsylvania to begin a new life with the people who had sponsored us. There was a man on that plane who smoked the most terrible smelling cigar, and I got so sick from the odor of his cigar that I was afraid my baby was going to be born on that plane!

Our sponsors' names were Fred and Florence Halstead. They lived in a mansion up on a hill and let us stay in a little house at the bottom of the hill.

Our son, Bobby, was born the 24th of October in 1954, on our first anniversary, in Elwood City, Pennsylvania. Our family doctor's name was Dr. Wilson. I still remember him vividly. We stayed in that little house for awhile, and since we weren't accustomed to fancy things, we were quite content there.

Eventually we bought a 95 acre farm in Fombel, just about two miles from where our sponsors, the

Halstead's lived. It was just beautiful. We raised white-faced Hereford beef cattle. We had 65 heads, our own bull, seven ponies, a big beautiful German shepherd dog named Rex, and a cat named Princess.

One summer our cat had seven kittens. I used to walk about one-half hour to a millionaire's mansion to clean it once a week. That cat and her seven little kittens would walk with me and wait outside for four hours while I cleaned the house, and then walked back home with me.

Our farm had a wooded area with a little creek running through, a magnificent hill for pasture and flat land for fields. Slowly we bought all the machinery and small farm equipment we needed.

I worked at the Howard Johnson Restaurant right on the Ohio and Pennsylvania border for nine and one-half years, cleaned a millionaire's place, and took care of our place.

During those years, we gradually remodeled the old farmhouse, which proved to be quite an undertaking! There were at least 12 rolls of wallpaper that had to be taken off the walls. It was a mess!

When my husband, whose name was Reinhart, came home from work, we would eat supper together, and then I would go to work at Howard Johnson's from 4:45 until midnight while he stayed with Bobby. I worked so hard, but I loved our beautiful farm. We attended church in Beaver Falls, Pennsylvania, about 15 or 20 miles from where we lived.

Bobby was six years old when he first drove a tractor. I would ride on the wagon. My husband would put the bales of hay on the wagon, I would stack them, and then we all unloaded them to the hayloft in the barn. It took all three of us working together to make it all work.

After we had been married for about ten years, my Aunt Mary (one of my mother's sisters), her oldest daughter Clara and her husband Frank, along with her youngest daughter Irene and her husband Rudy came from Canada to visit us. They came in on a Wednesday evening by car.

At that same time, my youngest sister came to America to stay with us. I thought it would be nice to have somebody here from my family and looked forward to her visit. On the same Wednesday evening when our company was coming in from Canada, I was on my way to pick up my sister from New York.

I had all kinds of food prepared and the freezer all stocked in preparation for our company. They stayed for ten days and we had a great time. I kept busy cooking, grilling and taking care of my guests.

When my Canadian company left that Friday, my

Aunt Mary cried and said, "Paula, we'll be praying for you and I am very, very sorry for you." I wondered what she was talking about, but just left it at that.

Bobby always had to get up early and walk down the hill about a tenth of a mile to catch the school bus. But one day, when our Canadian visitors had been gone about a week, Bobby started complaining to me that he just didn't want to get up in the mornings. He kept saying that he just didn't feel good. This was very rare for Bobby to feel this way and I was confused about what was wrong.

Apparently my company and my son had seen and sensed trouble that I was totally oblivious to. I slept every night like a log because I was so tired from working hard every day. It seemed I never had an idle minute. When I wasn't working, I was crocheting, making dolls and pillows, sold dozens and dozens of all sorts of handmade crafts to pay for remodeling our beautiful farmhouse and buying furniture, rugs, and curtains. I had worked so hard and invested so much of myself into our farm and our lives together. As it turned out, I was losing my husband, our farm and dreams. I was in total shock.

The whole story of what happened is just too ugly for words and would cause pain to the innocent involved so I will just say that Bobby and I moved to a little house about two miles away from the farm.

The last time Bobby and I went back down the hill from the farm, it almost broke my heart. The cattle came to the fence when I called them and the little calves were jumping they were so happy to see me, as I was to see them.

It was during this time that my weight went from 128 pounds down to 93 pounds. I was completely exhausted from working and dealing with this situation.

Sometime in May, it was real chilly and I got up

during the night to go to the bathroom. I stopped by Bobby's room to cover him up more and when I went back to my bedroom, I fainted and fell. That woke Bobby up. I think it was 3:00 in the morning. I was completely unconscious for a long time. Bobby went to the neighbors and they called Dr. Wilson. Dr Wilson came, and of course I didn't know anything about all that. They tell me the ambulance came and took me to Elwood City Hospital. I woke up on the way and since the roof of the ambulance was so low and close to my face, I thought I was in a casket. The driver and attendant were so nice and reassuring to me. They told me I was not in a casket, but in an ambulance, and then turned on the siren so I could here it.

I was in the hospital for five weeks with a complete breakdown. A lady from my church, named Sandy Dancek had a son named Eddie who was a little younger than Bobby and she took Bobby to her house and cared for him while I was in the hospital. (Thank you Sandy!)

I finally recuperated and was released from the hospital. I decided to look for a job and got one right away working at a factory in Elwood City making men's clothing.

We moved to Elwood City, about 20 miles or so from the farm and rented a small apartment above a Jewish department store. Bobby attended school there in Elwood City and as time went by, we grew to be content there.

The manager of the factory where I worked was a little Jewish man. He was mean to some people and I got into it with him one day. I said, "You know what? You are like Hitler. Why are you so mean to people?" He didn't answer.

There were tables about 25 feet long on which I had to stack 20 pieces of material to exactness, like a deck of cards. Some were heavy and some were lighter cloth. The heavier cloth was very hard to stack like that. One lady who worked there couldn't come in for a week or so because of an illness, and the manager asked me if I wanted to try to do her job in the cutting room where she had worked.

I would be required to draw the pattern on top of the material and cut it with a cutter knife about a yard high. Then I would have to zigzag with the machine according to the pattern. The first time I did it, I was afraid of ruining all that material. I knew that would get me in great trouble. But the several dozen I had cut at one time all came out perfect. He asked me if I would like to stay on the cutting machine. I asked if I would get more money and he said yes. So I agreed to stay there.

One day there were a couple of visitors coming from another company. While I was cutting, I had to watch what I was doing and not look anywhere else, otherwise I would ruin the whole stack of patterns. I didn't notice, but my co-worker said my boss and the visitors were watching me. I didn't look; I just kept working like they weren't even there. She told me several times that they were still watching me.

I found out later that those visitors said they had never seen anything like it. What I say is the truth. So I must have been good at cutting the patterns. I liked the job, but some of the material was very hard to stack so high and so precisely since the texture was not always even and was often crinkled. Nonetheless, I stayed there for quite awhile.

Chapter Ten

Columbus, Indiana

In the summer of 1969, Bobby and I moved to Columbus, Indiana, with only $300. I found work right away at Sap's Bakery and in the fall Bobby went to Columbus North High School. He worked every day after school for two hours at Sap's, checking the machines to make sure they were clean and working properly and I worked on the production line. There was a gentleman by the name of Eric Grimm who was the manager. We made millions of donuts every week.

We had a good time during those years. We lived very simply, saved our money and bought a little house where I still live and which I refer to as my

"Little Shanty."

Bobby graduated with honors from the Columbus North High School in 1972, which at that time was the largest class of students ever to graduate from that school. He was among the top 10 academic honor students. The local newspaper had an article on the front page featuring the three girls and seven boys who comprised the top ten students that year, complete with pictures and stories of those students. His graduation event was a very festive occasion for us, as you can imagine.

We learned in 1973 that Bobby's father had passed away in Pennsylvania.

During the summer months while Bobby was still in high school, he worked at a construction company. In the fall after his high school graduation, he went to Andrews University in Michigan for a year. Picking him up and taking him back on weekends and holidays was a long commute, and we just couldn't afford another car at that time. So, he enrolled at Indiana University in Bloomington which was much closer to our home, and began his sophomore year there.

He was in Pre-Med for the first three years, then he changed his course of study to Natural Resources. When President Reagan was elected to office during that time, he abolished a lot of the natural resource governmental positions. Bobby feared he would not be able to find employment in that field, so he again changed his major, this time to microbiology. In 1976, he graduated from Indiana University with a degree in microbiology. He now works for the city of Columbus in the utilities laboratory.

He worked so hard during those years, going to school, working after school and summers, plus staying on top of his studies. We both worked hard, and we finally made it. He had completed college and was on the road to a wonderful career in Columbus, Indiana, for which I am so thankful.

From Sap's, I went to the Holiday Inn and worked as a hostess and supervisor. Charlie Brown was the manager and I liked the job very much. However, there were certain things that made me feel uncomfortable, so I decided to move on.

In September of 1972, I started working at Cummins Engine Company, where I worked for ten years and retired in 1983. I kept busy during that time. I loved to entertain and would have lots of people to my house for dinner.

I have been involved with our local Seventh Day Adventist Church here in Columbus for years. I was here when it still was on the corner of 19th and Elm Street and then we built a new church at 2909 Talley road in Columbus.

Columbus, Indiana, has been a wonderful place

to live and I have been quite happy here. I have seen many changes through the years in our community. As everything else in the United States, and really the whole world, life is more complicated than it used to be.

There seems to be so much chaos everywhere in the whole world. Of course, that is a prophecy in the Bible, and we're told that's the way it is going to be in the end times. The way adults and young people behave, the terrible world-wide disasters we witness happening everyday, have all been prophesized to happen before the coming of the Lord Jesus Christ to finally take his people home. I pray for every soul to be ready for the Lord's coming because I feel it is going to be very soon. I have lived through so much, have seen some pretty horrendous happenings, but I feel terrible times are ahead of us. The Bible refers to it as "troubled times like never before on this earth." Don't you think that is something for all of us to think about?

Well, Bobby is now married to a wonderful lady named Debbie. Together they are raising two grandchildren and doing a good job, the best they can. The Lord will repay them for that, I'm sure. I do hope they will all come to church soon and serve the Lord the way we all should serve him. The Bible says it is our duty to love God, do good to others, and love our neighbors. That is what I am trying to do, as best I can.

I have lost a lot of money in my life and a lot of people have taken advantage of me. But the Lord was good to Bobby and me. We had hard times, but we made it. Thanks Bobby, I'm very sorry you had to go through so many blunders with me!

On May 25, 2005, I was driving home from cleaning the beautiful house of my friends, Mr. and Mrs. Beck, who lived west of Columbus. I was eastbound on State Road 46 going toward the new bridge into Columbus. I had the green light, but a man driving the other vehicle ran a red light and must have been driving too fast. Before I knew what was happening, my car was broadsided and I was involved in a terrible accident. It was just awful. I felt sorry for him, but as a result of this accident, my whole life has changed.

Prior to my accident in 2005, I was in excellent shape physically. I hadn't been to a doctor for 23 years, except for routine check-ups and once when I cut my finger on a lawn mower.

This accident, though, has very adversely altered my health and therefore my entire life. It has just been terrible. I used to walk on all my errands and hardly ever used my car, but now am seldom able to walk anywhere.

I have become dependent on others and this, plus

not being nearly as productive as I used to be, have been difficult adjustments to make. All I know is that I wasn't sick at all before the automobile accident, but now I'm in nearly constant pain and have a lot of sleepless nights. But I have to keep trucking the best I can, and trust in the Lord to take care of me as he promised in His Word that He will "never leave you or forsake you."

I am thankful for all those years when I had felt so good and had what I considered a good life. I had a beautiful garden with lots of fruit, flowers and vegetables, and enjoyed my life and independence. I still worked hard, was able to help other people, and among other activities was privileged to teach a German class for five years at the ABC Learning Center in Columbus. Through this teaching experience, I came to know a lot of very nice people in Columbus. We would have beautiful programs at Christmas time and before summer vacation at the school. It was so enjoyable working with those children and getting to know many of the prominent people in town.

PAULA WITH SOME OF HER GERMAN CLASS STUDENTS AT THE ABC LEARNING CENTER IN COLUMBUS, INDIANA

When I was still working, I would travel on my vacations and I'm so glad I did, because nobody can take that away from me.

Chapter Eleven
Visiting Home Again

In 1964, when Bobby was about ten years old, we went back to visit my home country. That time we traveled by train in Germany across the border into East Germany which was still under Communism. Travel in the Communist countries was especially bad. A lot of people would go visiting by train, which was allowed if we had our papers prepared weeks ahead of time.

On the train the travelers would sing and laugh and talk, but the minute we crossed the border into a Communist country, it was like we went through a tunnel into a big morgue. No one would say a thing, just look at each other. The towns were dirty and drab and the weeds were growing higher than the windows. Apparently nobody did a thing to keep up the land. Everything was dilapidated. The roads had huge holes. This was my first time back and it was just unbelievable.

We crossed Checkpoint Charley in Berlin and went through six checkpoints. At every point, about ten miles apart, they would take every single thing out of our suitcases.

In those days, pantyhose were new on the market and had just become famous, so I took 15 pair with me to give to my family.

I had never made a cake from a boxed cake mix in my life, but this was a novelty in East Germany, so I took five of those with me so I could show them to my family.

We never had commercial toilet paper when I grew up. We used any kind of paper we could get and cut it up in pieces for our toilet paper. So I also included several rolls for my family. The guards at the checkpoints didn't confiscate anything, but just threw everything around.

At the last checkpoint I said to one of the guards, "Would you like a pair of pantyhose for your wife or a boxed cake mix or toilet paper?" He looked around, then looked at me and said, "Ma'am, I would sure love to, but I'd better not."

First we went to Czechoslovakia to our old homestead where my Uncle Martin was still living. He didn't leave with my father and the other men when they had been evacuated that November in 1944. We found out that his own cousin had betrayed him, and as a result he had been badly beaten and imprisoned when the Communists invaded our old homestead.

It was about a mile from the railroad station to my Uncle Martin's home. Bobby had his suitcase and I had mine and they were pretty heavy because of all that I had packed, but we walked the distance to their house. I hadn't seen them since Easter in 1944.

We got there about 20 minutes before Uncle Martin was to come home from work for lunch, so we put a roll of our toilet paper in the outside toilet (they didn't have indoor plumbing yet). Well, he went to the outside bathroom before coming in for lunch and when he came in he said, "Boy, my rear-end probably thought it was its birthday." We all cracked up laughing! We had a really good visit together.

Then Bobby, my Aunt Mary from Canada, and I traveled to Mecklenburg over by the East Sea to visit her sister who was my mother, my only brother, and my sister, Bertha. My mother and father lived the rest of their lives in the same little place over the hog pen where they had been taken after leaving the refugee camp in Schmollnitz.

When I saw my dad he said, "How can you travel by yourself all over the world?"

I said, "Well, I wanted to see you. Aren't you glad to see me again?"

He didn't say anything. As I said before, they are funny people, not mean really, just different. There was no love or caressing, just nothing. After we were grown, my siblings and I wondered how those two people could have so many children without ever showing any love.

They picked us up from the train station in the most dilapidated truck you ever saw. My aunt Mary rode in the cab with the driver to the village where my folks, my brother and his family, and some cousins lived. Bobby and I rode in the back of the truck. The holes in road were so deep that by the time we got to our destination, we were not only black and blue, but since it also was pouring rain, we were also filthy and wet. Our suitcases were drenched. Finally we got there and Bobby cried and said, "I want to go back home!"

I told him we wouldn't stay there long. We ended up staying about ten days. I probably would have stayed a little longer, but the way things were, there was hardly anything to eat. One day there was some commotion and everyone was running through the village. Bobby just looked at me.

"There's chicken today and a quarter pound of butter!" So we all walked an hour and a-half to the next little village where the chicken and butter was and stood in line for two and one-half hours; but when our time came, there was no chicken and no butter available – there was nothing left.

Can you imagine me and Bobby coming from America to this? Especially Bobby. He had never seen such a thing or experienced a scarcity of food in his short lifetime. And those chickens they were selling looked almost green. Some people said they cooked them for hours and they still looked like leather and had no taste.

So we walked the one and a half hour journey back home. My family had a little garden with potatoes and a nearby farmer had given us some milk. We baked some bread and had that with some potatoes and milk.

Bobby was so glad when we got over the border again, through that dark tunnel and back to the other side. Everybody was singing, laughing, jumping around and shouting how good it was to be back and to be free again.

Paula's mother and father

In 1968, on another trip to East Germany to visit my family, we rented a car. We would barely have our car parked before the police would be right there asking if we had a permit to be there, who we were visiting, and why. They demanded names, addresses, and everything.

I explained that we had just arrived there and that we were on vacation to look around and sightsee.

They said we had to have permission and gave us a hard time, but we finally got to go on our way. Coming from the freedom of America, Bobby was perplexed by all of this, of course. It was still the beautiful, beautiful countryside I remembered, but things were still so rundown and uncared for.

In the Communist countries, people were told when they could take a vacation, where they could go on their vacation, and how long they could be on vacation. They had nothing to say about it, no choice.

I had worn a blouse that was really pretty and soon realized that I shouldn't have worn that behind the Iron Curtain. One of the officers just could not get over that beautiful blouse. I said "I wish I had another blouse here, Sir. I would give this one to you for your wife." I guess that kind of disarmed him because he was nicer after I said that.

In 1989 I was visiting my sisters Irene and Klara in Illertissen, Bavaria, about an hour drive from Stuttgart where the airport is. I heard that my brother from East Germany was going to come and visit. At that time a husband and wife from the Communist East Germany weren't allowed to travel together to the West on a vacation. Only one or the other could go so that the government could be sure the one going would come back. So my brother came to visit without his wife.

One evening during our visit together, my brother-in-law, Irvin, Irene's husband, turned on the television for the evening news at 6:00. On this broadcast, they showed the Iron Wall being torn down. People were hacking at the wall and screaming, yelling, laughing and singing. I said to my brother, "Martin, by the time you go back home there won't be any checkpoints! You will be a free man!"

He said, "No, I can't believe it!" He had spent all his life living under Communism. He just could not believe it.

I assured him that it was right there on the television, so it had to be true! The rest of us just had a ball! We danced around and laughed and rejoiced. But he was so stunned that he couldn't even move. He just couldn't believe that he was finally going to be free and that he and his wife would be able to take their next vacation together wherever they wanted to go.

What an unbelievable sight it was to see Reagan say to Gorbachev, "Mr. Gorbachev, tear down that wall!" And he did, and I will never forget that happy day with my only brother!

I have seen so many, many remarkable changes in my lifetime! I recall when we first put electricity in the barn at home, how when we heard the first airplane overhead and the whole town would run out to see it. I remember sometime in the 1920's when a boy graduated from high school and went out and bought an old dilapidated taxi. He brought it back to our town and we saw a vehicle for the first time.

Today, nearly 100 years later, look where we are now! We're flying over the ocean. I have flown many, many times and am still amazed that within eight hours I am across the world.

It is quite a different world. I have seen it all, have gone through it all, and stand in amazement. Here it is 2007 and I am still here. "This is a miracle" I say to the Lord.

From Zipserland to West Germany to Canada to Pennsylvania to Indiana and back to my beloved homeland is roughly 10,000 miles.

Nobody knows exactly why my forefathers

migrated from Saxony in East Germany to a beautiful valley in little Slovakia called Zipserland where **MY AMAZING LIFE** began January 30th, 1921.

My mother named me "**PAULA**" which means "small." I am barely five feet tall and weigh about 100 pounds.

My father always had faith that I could handle any situation and said I was never afraid of anything. My life has offered many challenges to that bravery, and it seems I have one last battle to test my courage: I have been told I have leukemia.

My life has often been harsh and hard, and there were so many times I felt alone in wondering which way to turn and what to do. But the Lord has gently yet firmly led me all the way, and I trust Him completely to either grant me one more miracle, this time the miracle of healing my leukemia, or to carry me one more mile across one last bridge, happily and safely to His Other Side.

After all, what's one more mile to Him who has already given me

TEN THOUSAND MILES OF MIRACLES

through

BOMBS, BUNKERS, BAYONETS, THE BIG BROWN HOUSE, A LITTLE ITALIAN BOAT, A DEVASTATING BETRAYAL, MANY, MANY BLESSINGS, AND NOW A BOOK?

...The End(?)

Time will tell.....

A TRIBUTE TO MY GOD!

What should I thank you for Lord?

First of all, I'd like to thank you for your holy word.

Thank you for bringing me through another week,

For this your holy Sabbath day, which for me is a treat

For this beautiful place of worship, you have given us

Indeed I'd like to thank you very, very much.

I'd like to thank you for the sunshine and the rain,

For the knowledge from your holy word I gain.

Thank you for coming to save me, dear Lord,

For the plan of salvation you gave in your word.

Thank you for the strength you give me for each day

For helping me walk the narrow way.

Thank you for walking for me that path of sorrow,

For your love toward me, for a better tomorrow.

Lord, there are so many things each day to be thankful for,

Your blessings toward me are every day more and more.

You are so loving and kind toward me all the time,

Please help to walk in your ways so sublime.

Thank you Lord, for the birds, and the grass, and the flowers,

Thank you for keeping me, and watching over me every hour.

Thank you for shelter and clothing and food you provide,

For your great love and mercy, that in Thee I can

hide.

Thank you Lord for helping me each trial to bear,

For your coming I'll be ready, and "Well done" I may hear.

Please keep me and help me, and save me from all sin,

Keep me faithful and true, so in Your kingdom I may go in.

--by Paula Lindemann

The following true story had been told around Europe after the war. I had often wished I could remember exactly how it went. Then one day, almost fifty years later, I received a newsletter in the mail from our church and there was that story in print that I had wished I could remember! When the story first came out during WWII, the exact location was not revealed because of the safety of the people involved. I believe this took place in East Germany. I must share it with you.

A MIRACLE OF FAITH

Do you believe in God's word?

An active Christian worker, in a certain European country, had been arrested and imprisoned for his faith. Shortly after his arrest, he was taken from the prison cell and led into a secret police interrogation room. There he found a secret police officer, a KGB (a Communist secret service agent), and a doctor sitting at the interrogation table. Lying open on the table was a Bible.

The Christian prisoner was ordered to take a seat and the interrogation began. He was asked, "Do you believe that this is God's Word?"

He answered, "Yes."

The secret police official then asked him to read a certain verse. It was Mark 16:18. The Christian read, "And if they drink any deadly thing, it shall not hurt them."

"Do you believe this part of the Bible, too?" the officer demanded.

The Christian replied, "Yes."

The officer than placed a filled glass on the table, explaining, "In this glass there is a strong poison. If the book is true as you insist, it won't hurt you. To show you we aren't playing with you, watch this."

The officer brought in a large dog and had the dog drink of the liquid. In a very few moments, the dog was lying dead on the floor.

The officer looked at the Christian and asked, "Do you still claim this book you call 'God's Word' is true?"

The Christian again answered, "Yes, it is God's Word, and it is true."

"Then drink the entire glass!" shouted the Communist officer, with the doctor looking on.

The Christian then knew that this was the supreme test of his faith. He asked for permission to pray before drinking, and they granted him permission. He knelt down before the table, took the glass in his hand, and prayed for his family, that they might remain steadfast in their faith.

He prayed for the Communist officer and the doctor that they might find God and become Christians also.

Then closing his prayer, he prayed, "Oh Lord, Thou seest how they have challenged Thee. I am ready to die, but I believe in Thy word, that nothing shall happen to me. Should you plan differently, I am ready to meet Thee. My life is in your hands. May Thy will be done."

With that, he lifted the glass and drank it

down. The Communist officer and the doctor were surprised. They did not expect him to do this, feeling he would break first. They waited for him to collapse, as had the dog. But moments passed into minutes. Minutes seemed to be hours. With complete silence in the room, everyone was waiting for the inevitable death.

Then, after several long minutes, the doctor made the first move. He took the arm of the Christian and felt his pulse. It was normal. He looked for other symptoms. There were none. Expressing amazement and astonishment, he continued his examination, but could find no trace of harm whatsoever. As the examination continued, the doctor became more amazed. Finally he slumped into his seat, paused a moment, reached into his pocket, and removed his Communist Party card, tore it in half and threw it on the floor. Then he reached out for the Bible, held it and said, "From today, I will also believe this book. It must be true. I too am ready to believe this Christ who did this thing before my eyes!"

---Copied

Printed in the United States
201932BV00001B/136-288/P

To Barbara & Carrol
Summer !

From
Pauley